Growing Things

Catching Sunlight

A Book About Leaves

Written by Susan Blackaby
Illustrated by Charlene DeLage

Content Adviser: Jeffrey H. Gillman, Ph.D., Assistant Professor
Horticultural Science, University of Minnesota, St. Paul, Minnesota

Reading Adviser: Susan Kesselring, M.A., Literacy Educator
Rosemount-Apple Valley-Eagan (Minnesota) School District

PICTURE WINDOW BOOKS
Minneapolis, Minnesota

Editor: Nadia Higgins
Designer: Nathan Gassman
Page production: Picture Window Books
The illustrations in this book were painted with watercolor.

Picture Window Books
5115 Excelsior Boulevard
Suite 232
Minneapolis, MN 55416
1-877-845-8392
www.picturewindowbooks.com

Printed in the United States of America.
1 2 3 4 5 6 08 07 06 05 04 03

Library of Congress Cataloging-in-Publication Data
Blackaby, Susan.
Catching sunlight : a book about leaves / written by Susan Blackaby ; illustrated by Charlene DeLage.
v. cm. — (Growing things)
Contents: Leaves making food—Leaves in spring—Leaves in summer—Leaves in autumn—All kinds of leaves—
Leaf seasons—Fun facts—Comparing leaves.
ISBN 1-4048-0111-1 (lib. bdg.)
1. Leaves—Juvenile literature. [1. Leaves.] I. DeLage, Charlene, 1944- ill. II. Title.
QK649 .B62 2003
575.5'7—dc21
2002156332

Table of Contents

Leaves Making Food

Walk through a garden. Hike in the woods. Run across a soccer field.

When you step outdoors, plants with green leaves are all around you. Every green leaf you see is busy making food.

5

Leaves make food through photosynthesis.
During photosynthesis, leaves soak up sunlight.
The energy from the sunlight
is stored inside the leaves.

Leaves take in carbon dioxide from the air. They get water from the soil. They use the energy from the sun to turn the carbon dioxide and water into sugar. At the same time, the leaves give off the oxygen we need to breathe.

Leaves in Spring

You cannot see how leaves make food, but you can see clues through the year. The clues show you that leaves are hard at work.

In the spring, the days get warmer. Sunlight lasts longer.

Leaves poke up through the soil and open on the ends of the stems.

Leaves come to life after the quiet winter. They start making food the plant needs.

Leaves in Summer

Through the long, warm summer days, the leaves keep making food.
Food that isn't used right away is stored in the stem and roots of the plant.

The food is used to make the plant grow healthy and strong. Its flowers bloom. Its seeds develop in fruits and pods. Its stems get bigger.

Leaves in Autumn

In autumn, the days get shorter and the nights get cooler. There is less and less sunlight and water for photosynthesis. The leaves stop making food.

In some plants, the leaves lose their green color.
They change to red, gold, yellow, orange, and brown.
When the cold weather comes, the leaves drop to the ground.

Evergreen plants have tough leaves with a waxy coating.

The leaves do not dry out in cold weather.

The plants stay green all winter.

Evergreen Plants

Cedar	Pine
Spruce	Redwood
Fir	Holly
Bamboo	Camellia
Lavender	Heather

Evergreen plants do lose their leaves,

but they do not lose them all at the same time.

Every few years, the oldest leaves fall to make room for new growth.

All Kinds of Leaves

Leaves come in different sizes and shapes.

Leaf shape can be used to help tell plants apart.

Oaks and maples are both big trees, but their leaves are not the same.

16   Maple leaves are wide like the palm of your hand.

Oaks have groups of shiny leaves with thorny edges or large leaves with rounded edges.

Some plants are even named for their leaves:

- Bigleaf dogwood
- Fiddleleaf fig
- Arrow-leaved ash
- Silver-leaved poplar
- Sword-leaf fern

17

Leaves take care of plants' needs wherever they live.

In the shade, plants may have very big leaves or stems with many little leaves to soak up as much sunlight as possible.

In the desert, leaves may be fat and fleshy to store plenty of water.

Spikes and prickles keep away thirsty insects, birds, and animals.

Scales

Needles

Some evergreen leaves look like tiny scales wrapped around a stem.

Some look like needles. The spiky needles can be sharp.

They have a strong, sweet, piney smell.

The smell keeps away hungry insects and animals.

19

Leaves can be smooth, hairy, waxy, prickly, fleshy, or scaly.

Leaves can be silver, purple, blue, gray, and all shades of green.

Leaves can be huge fans or tiny blades.

Over your head and under your feet, every green leaf is soaking up sunlight.
Leaves are working to keep the planet covered with plants.

Leaf Seasons

Cut a leaf shape out of paper.
Color one side of the leaf green to show how it looks in spring and summer.
Color the other side of the leaf to show how the color changes in autumn.
Write this poem on the green side:
Green leaves spring to life in the Spring!
Write this poem on the other side:
Leaves lose green color in the Fall and fall!

Fun Facts

- Leaves that fall to the ground break down and turn into rich soil.
- Leaves that fall to the ground help keep plant roots warm during the winter.
- Dark green lettuce leaves have more vitamins than light green lettuce leaves.
- Plants that grow near city streetlights may keep their leaves longer than plants growing in the country.
- Some people say that the four leaves of a four-leaf clover stand for Faith, Hope, Love, and Luck.
- A rainy summer and dry fall with sunny days and cool nights will bring the brightest autumn color.

Words to Know

autumn—the season of the year between summer and winter, also called fall

carbon dioxide—gas in the air that is breathed out of people's and animals' lungs

evergreen—a plant that has green leaves or needles all year round

needle—the thin, pointed leaf of a fir or pine

photosynthesis—a process plants use to make food and oxygen

scale—the thin, overlapping leaf of some evergreens

Comparing Leaves

This diagram compares evergreen leaves and non-evergreen leaves.
How are they alike? How are they different?

Evergreens

- Thick, waxy leaves (can be like needles or scales)
- Leaves hold moisture through winter
- Leaves stand up to cold temperatures

Both

- Leaves use sunlight, water, and air to make food for the plant
- Leaves make oxygen for us to breathe

Non-Evergreens

- Flat, thin leaves of all shapes and sizes
- Leaves stop making food in autumn when days get shorter and cooler
- Leaves lose their green color and turn red, gold, orange, and brown
- Leaves fall off trees; trees are bare until new growth in spring

To Learn More

At the Library

Hall, Zoe. *Fall Leaves Fall!* New York: Scholastic Press, 2000.
Marzollo, Jean. *I Am a Leaf!* New York: Scholastic Press, 1998.
Saunders-Smith, Gail. *Leaves.* Mankato, Minn.: Pebble Books, 1998.
Ward, Kristin. *Leaves.* New York: PowerKids Press, 2000.

On the Web

Backyard Jungle
http://www.backyardjungle.org
A forum for kids to share their outdoor discoveries

EPA Kids' Site
http://www.epa.gov/kids
For information about exploring and protecting nature

Want more information about leaves? FACT HOUND offers a safe, fun way to find Web sites. All of the sites on Fact Hound have been researched by our staff. Simply follow these steps:

1. Visit *http://www.facthound.com.*
2. Enter a search word or 1404801111.
3. Click Fetch It.

Your trusty Fact Hound will fetch the best sites for you!

Index